Malik's Letter

Written by:
STONE RAMSEY

Illustrated by:
VLADIMIR CEBU, LL.B.

"Malik, you got a letter from your Dad."

"I don't want to read it."

"Why not. You usually enjoy reading his letters"

There was a brief silence,
then he mustered up a response.

MALIK: "Mommy. the kids are teasing me, because Dad's in jail."

"Well... Malik," said his mom. "your father is a good man, who may have made a **mistake**, yet he's working hard to never be away from his family again."

Malik began to straighten up his posture.

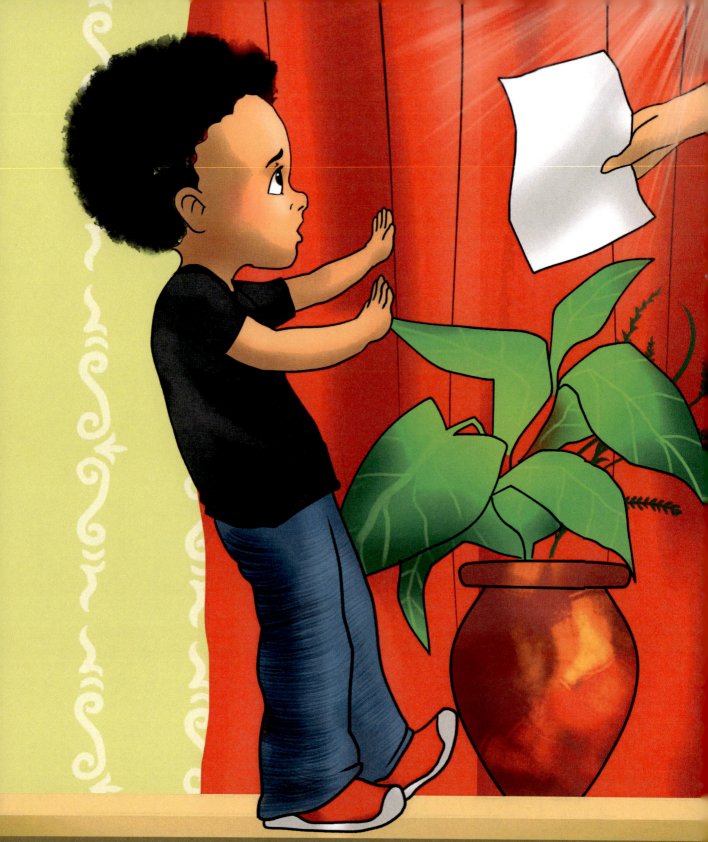

"But, the kids say, Dad is the kinda bird,
th-that don't fly. ...a Jailbird!"

"Your father loves you" ... she pleaded.

MALIK: "If he loved me, he wouldn't be in prison."

"Now, Malik," said his mother.

"Just because you make a mistake doesn't make you a bad person."

"Have you ever heard of Martin Luther King?
Or Malcolm X?"

"Yes." nodded Malik.

Well, both have been imprisoned,
even the great Nelson Mandela,
went from a prison cell, to a presidency, in South Africa.

"Do you think Dad, will become a president?"

"I can't tell you what your Dad will be, but one thing
I can tell you, is that he'll always love you,
and he'll work hard a being the best possible version of himself."

"Thank you, mommy.
I can't wait to go to school, now!"

What Zone am I in?

Blue	Green	Yellow	Red
Sad Sick Tired Bored Moving Slowly	Happy Calm Okay Focused Ready to Learn	Frustrated Worried Silly/Wiggly Excited Some Loss of Control	Mad/Angry Terrified Yelling/Hitting Elated Out of Control

I can try these tools:

walk

drink

break

Take deep breath
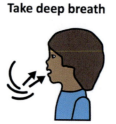

I can try these tools:

hug

Talk to an adult

break

Listen to music

I can try these tools:

walk

Can I solve my problem?

break

Take deep breath
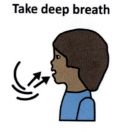

ALL ABOUT

I am ◯ years old

I Live with

My Friends Are

in

I like to watch

Favorite activities

My Favorite:

COLOR:_____

FOOD:_____

ANIMAL:_____

BOOKS:

I am good at

When I grow up
I want to be...

WE STAND TOGETHER AGAINST RACISM AND INTOLERANCE.

Different

Individuals

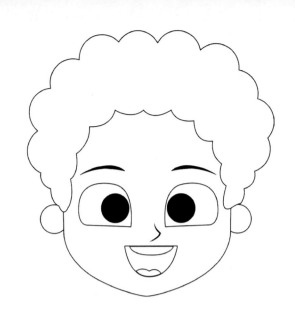

Valuing

Each other

Regardless of

Skin,

Intellect,

Talent or

Years

Malik's Letter

Oakland Author Stone Ramsey hits home and your heart with his new book, "Malik's Letter."

Sean "Stone" Ramsey, the Founder of the W.I.S.E. Program (The Written In Stone Entrepreneurship Program), a program that educates youth and adults on the independent aspects of Music and Publishing Industries as well as Entrepreneurship and Life skills. Author Stone Ramsey has an extensive background and experience in Business as well as the Arts & Entertainment Industry. He is the CEO of Ramsey Media Group, Founder of All Bay News Magazine, (the #1 Magazine in the Bay Area), and Author of 7 Urban Literature books, coined; "Hip-Hop" Lit.

Author Stone Ramsey was born and raised on the mean streets of Oakland, California. He could have become just another statistic, if not for his iron will and strong determination to succeed. As a youth, growing up during turbulent times, he struggled to find his path. After spending 16 years of his life in prison, he discovered his passion in Hip-Hop as well as writing. Author Stone Ramsey's life-story is remarkable and truly inspiring for any person, young or old. He was able to overcome marginalization and sub-par education to become a coveted Industry Mogul as well as an important Leader in the Community.

Made in the USA
Middletown, DE
30 January 2025

70588037R00015